DORSET AS SHE WUS

A guide to the Dorset dialect by Jean Bellamy

Local titles by the same author
Treasures of Dorset (1991)
A Dorset Quiz Book (1995)
A Second Dorset Quiz Book (1997)
The Dorset Tea Trail (1999)

S B Publications
19 Grove Road, Seaford,
East Sussex BN25 1TP
01323 893498

© 2002 Jean Bellamy

ISBN 185770 253 0

Drawings by Helen Fenton

Typeset by JEM Editorial
Printed and bound by
Tansleys Printers
19 Broad Street, Seaford
East Sussex BN25 1LS
01323 891019

Title page picture: Stoke Abbott

Contents

Introduction	3
Dictionary of Dorset dialect	6
A passel of trades	63
Old Dorset sayings	70
Dorset's dialect greats	76
A Dorset miscellany	84
Some Dorset delicacies	97
'Neath the Clavy	105
Dree Darset men in Lon'on	110
Two letters in dialect	114
Acknowledgments	118
About the author	119

Introduction

Researching old Dorset words is a fascinating – and often amusing - undertaking. Dialect adds character to a county with the use of words and phrases which are often so much more descriptive than standard English. Dorset has William Barnes, the county's much-loved poet, to thank for the fact that its dialect has been preserved in its entirety.

Generally speaking, Dorset dialect consists of old-fashioned words that are Anglo-Saxon in origin, most of which have ceased to be in general use, although some have continued to the present time. It is difficult to say when dialect words were first used and, of course, their creation has been a continuous process. Obviously some of the words were in fairly general use, though many others were found in some parts of the county more than others. It was the advent of schooling for everyone, and later the wireless, which caused the use of dialect to largely disappear.

Some dialect words are specific to certain towns, villages or trades, such as farming, fishing, brewing, spinning and weaving – and even to particular families, or just to children. Again, there are some Dorset dialect words which are similar to some used in other counties.

There was certainly a definite Dorset accent, although this varied in different parts of the county. The typical Dorset manner of speaking has a tendency to be in a slow tempo which gives the impression of diffidence, but is probably due to the fact that Dorset folk like to consider a situation at length before giving an opinion. With its

Ellen

soft and homely inflections, dialect words sometimes take on less abrasive meanings than words with the same meanings in standard English. With regard to the pronounciation, a, for example, is a sound between the a in 'late' and the e in 'meet', v is often used for f, and z is sometimes used for s.

I have recollections from the 1930s/50s of an elderly 'help' whom my parents employed once a week to assist with the cleaning of our large house. When my sister went off – somewhat reluctantly – to boarding-school, Ellen would say with a sad shake of her head, 'I think upon her every day!' Again, when enquiring as to someone's destination, she would ask, 'Where are you to?'

Many dialect words continued in use even after the distinctive accent began to disappear. Dorset dialect, I am told, was heard in Dorchester – and no doubt in many other places – as late as the 1960s. Even as recently as the 1980s, a farmer for whom I did some secretarial work always inserted a 'w' (following a consonant) into words such as hwome (home), or added a 'w' at the beginning of a word, as wold for 'old' – something which fell strangely on my ears, as I had not come across it before, even though I had lived in Dorset most of my life.

Obviously social status was a factor. Some folk had no knowledge at all of dialect while for others it was an intrinsic part of their childhood. Well-to-do families would have been quicker to adopt modern ways of speaking, looking upon the older dialect words as out of date and perhaps not very genteel.

This little book is not only a collection of Dorset dialect words, but also explores the wealth of treasure to be found among old Dorset sayings, saws, rhymes, letters, short stories, and even certain foods. It is also an opportunity to pay tribute to that notable early dialect collector and speaker, the poet William Barnes, as well as to two contemporary Dorset poets.

Any additions, corrections or comments with regard to Dorset dialect words will be very welcome from readers who may care to send them to me via the publisher.

Jean Bellamy, 2002

Dictionary of Dorset dialect

A

A-cothed – Rotten, or disease in the liver.
Aggy – Cornery, with sharp-looking joints. Very thin man.
To gather eggs (such as pheasant's) in the laying season.
A'gean/agien – Against.
Aish – The ash tree.
A'lass'n – Lest.
Amper – Pustules. *The chile is all out in an amper.*
Anby – Soon, bye-and-bye.
Ankly – The ankle.
Annan – *What did you say?*
A-pisty-pol – A mode of carrying a child, his legs on one's shoulders and his arms around one's neck or shoulders.
A'ra – Ever a. *Have ye met a'ra bwoy wi' a dog? He zent a cherry without a'ra stwone.*
A'r'n – E'er a one.

Aish

A's'n – Ask him.
A-stogged – Having one's feet stuck into clay or dirt.
A-stooded – Wheels stuck fast in soft soil.
A-strout – Stretched out stiffly like frozen linen.
A-thirt – Athwart, across.
Atter – After.
Auverlook – To overlook, to look upon with evil eye.
Avore – Before.
A-vrightened – Frightened.
A-zew – Dry of milk.

ℬ

Back along – Time past.
Back'ards – Backwards.
Bade – Bed.
Baff – Bath.
Bandy-lags – Crooked legs, as a bandy.
Bareridge – To ride bareback without a saddle.
Bargen – A small farm or homestead.

Barnaby bright – Said of Barnabas-day, about the mid-summer solstice.
Barred – Borrowed.
Barton – Cattle-yard.
Baub – Bulb.
Beens – Because – *I can't do it today beens I must goo to town.*
Best – Excel, get the better of.
Bile – Boil.
Bin – Been.
Bisom – Besom.
Bissen – Be not.
Bist – Be you?
Bithywin (withwind) – Convolvulus, bindweed.
Bittle – Hammer. Also a beetle.
Bleare – Blare, low as a cow.
Brack – Breach.
Braed – Bread.
Breadf – Breadth.
Brick – Break.
Broff – Broth.
Brush/broush – Brushwood, small branches of twigs or tree.

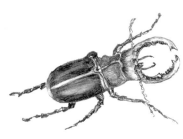

Bittle

8

Builded – Built (past tense).
Burry – Bury (or berry).
Bwoats – Boats/boots.
Bwoth – Both.
Bwoy – Boy.

C

Caddle – Entangle, muddle.
Cag-mag – Bad flesh meat.
Call hwome – Call banns in church.
Capple cow – Cow with white muzzle.
Car – Carry.
Carse – Course.
Ca's – Canst.
Cassen – Can'st not, can't.
Chammer – Chamber, bedroom.
Cheese-eater – Tom-tit so called for its cry.
Childag – Chilblain.
Chock-dog – An epithet bestowed on hard Dorset cheese.

Capple cow

Copsy – To cut tufts and thistles in field.
Couching – To pick couch.
Crip off – Pinch the stalk of a flower.
Criss-cross-lain – Christ-cross-line. The alphabet was formerly so called.
Critch – A bulging pitcher or big pan, as a butter critch.
Crock – A bulging iron pot.
Croopy – To sink one's body, bending the thighs down behind the legs.
Crowd – An apple-pie, apple cake. A fiddle.
Crowshell – Fresh water mussel shell.
Cruds – Curds.
Crump up – Bend or fold up, as if for warmth.
Cue – The shoe of an ox.
Cunnen man – A cunning man, a wizard.

Critch

D

Dadder, dather, dudder – Confound, bewilder.
Daffidown-dilly – Daffodil.
Dag, chilldag – Chilblain.

Dall it! – Confound it! (Dall is most likely a substitute for a swear word).

De-das – Simple, foolish, of inactive mind and body.

Disfugure – Disfigure.

Dolk-spitter – A tool for pulling or cutting up docks.

Dor – Dull, foolish. *That were dum and dor-* hence doormouse.

Doughbeaked – Half-witted, of weak or inactive mind.

Dout – To put out, extinguish.

Drabble-tail – Having one's gown-tail dirty.

Drub – Throb or beat. *My head do drub.*

Duck, duckish – Twilight. *In the duck of the even'en.*

Duddles – In the dods or dumps.

Dumby/Dubby topped – As a knife with a rounded or blunt top.

Dummer – Dust.

Dunducky – Of dim or dull hue, colourless.

Dunch-pudden – Hard or plain pudding of only flour or water without plums or suet.

Dungy – Downcast, dull, as spoken of a horse. Whence 'donkey'.

Daffidown-dilly

E

Eacor – Acorn.
Eacer – Acre.
Ees – Yes.
Eesterday – Yesterday.
Eer – Yet.
Eger, erger – Sharp, sour, as cider.
Elemen – Made of elm.
Elt – A young sow or pig.
    Em – Them.
       En – Him.
       Er – He.
       Eth – Earth.
       Eve – To become damp as a stone from condensation or vapour on its surface.
       Every/ever-grass – A species of grass/rye grass.

Elt

Eacor

F

Faddle – A pack, bundle.
Falter – To fail as a crop. *I be a-feard the teaties will falter.*
Feasen – Faces.
Figged-pudden – Plum pudding.
Fineg/finneg – Not to answer the call of duty. *You fineged.*
Flannen – Flannel.
Flinders – Flying bits as of a thing smashed.
Fling – To kick, spoken of a horse.
Flisky – Flying, as mist.
Flop – A mass of thin mud.
Flounce – A flinging or flying as of splashed water, or a falling into it.
Flump – A heavy flying fall.
Fob – The froth of the sea as it washed on the shore.
Fooch – To push, poke.
Footy – Little, insignificant.
Forefriends – Ancestors.
Foresters/forestylees – Horseflies.

Figged-pudden

Freemarten – Female calf of a twin, of which the other is a bull.
Frith/vrith – Brushwood.
Frog-hopper – Cicada.
Furmity – Frumenty.

G

Gad – A stake or bar of metal.
Gakey – One who gakes/gawks. A fool, a cuckoo.
Gally-crow – Scarecrow.
Gammen – Play or sport with one another.
Gap – Large breach in hedge, a small one being a shard.
Gapmouth – A nightjar.
Gawly – Applied to land spongy or wet.
Gay – Fresh or green. *That is too gay to carry yet.*
Geate – Gate.
Gee ho, go ho – Addressed to horses.
Giddygander – The early purple orchid and the green-winged meadow orchid, and other species of orchid (so called in Blackmore Vale).
Gi'e in – To give in, give up a contest.

Giddygander

Gi'e out – To give out, give up a pursuit. To fail. *My lags do gi'e out.*

Gil'cup/giltycup – Giltcup, buttercup.

Gilp – Boast.

Gimmy – Hinge of two parts, working on a joint.

Girt – Great.

Glean/glene – To sneer, smile jeeringly.

Gleare – To glaze, as tiles or bricks.

Glow/glaw/glawoo – To stare, to watch with fixed and wide-open eyes.

Glutch – Swallow, glut, gulp.

Gollikins/By Gollykins – An exclamation.

Goocoo – Cuckoo.

Goo wi'/goo after – To court. *He do go wi' Polly Hine.*

Goodhussy – Good housewife. Also a threadcase.

Good-now – Good neighbour.

Googary – Giddy, shaky.

Goold – Gold.

Golden-chain – Laburnum.

Goolden-drop – A variety of wheat.

Gossip – Godfather/mother. Also good friend.

Gil'cup

15

"When the warm sun that brings seed-time
And harvest, has returned again."

Longfellow.

Gout – Underwater gutter.
Grabble – To grab. *There, mother, I drapped my apples an' Jack grabbled them all up.*
Granf'er – Grandfather.
Granm'er – Grandmother.
Gribble – Young crabtree or blackthorn, or a knotty walking stick made of it.
Griddle – Grind corn very coarsely or imperfectly.
Grip – Handful of wheat.
Grotten – Sheep-slade, a run or pasture for sheep.
Groun' – Field. *Pleased down to groun* (Pleased to the very toes).
Grout – To grub or dig out a small ditch.
Gudgeon – Short forked stake used in hedging.
Guilder – An intermediate or subsidiary flow of the tide.
Gummy – Thick, clumsy, as a gummy ankle.
Gwain – Going.
Gwains on – Goings on, doings, or behaviour.

ℋ

Hacker – Broad hoe. To strike the teeth together in a shaking from cold or fear.
Hackle/bee-hackle – Sheaf of straw forming a cloak or roof over a beehive.

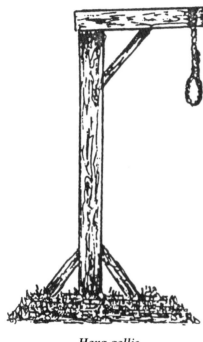

Hang-gallis

Hag-rod/rode/ridden – Nightmare attributed to the supernatural presence of a witch/hag by whom one is ridden in sleep.

Halterath – Bridle-path; a road for one on horse-back, but not for a carriage.

Ham/hamel – Enclosure.

Hamchaw – To hem and haw before giving an answer.

Hame, haulm – The hollow stalk of plants, as beanhame, peashame, teatyhame.

Handy – Useful; also near.

Hangen-house – A shed under a continuation of the roof of a house.

Hang-gallis – Hang-gallows, fit for the gallows. *A hang-gallis rogue.*

Han'sel – A hand gift, something given to a young woman at her wedding towards the housekeeping.

Hard – A hard boy is a big boy, hard being opposed to tender in a child of tender years.

Hardle – To entangle.

Hart-berry – Whortle-berry, bilberry.

Harvest-man – Cranefly/daddy-long-legs.

Ha'skin-cheese – Halfskin cheese, which is made of milk skimmed only once.

Haskets – Brushwood.

Hassen – Hast not.

Hassock/hassick – A tuft of sedge or brushwood.

Hatch – Wicket or little low grating on the gate, a half-door. Also hitch.

Hatches – Double gates.

Haves, heps – The fruit of the wild rose.

Hav – The spikelet of the oat. *The woats be out in hav.*

Hawked/howked cow – Cow with a white or white-patched face.

Haymaiden – Plant of the mint tribe, ground ivy, used for making a medicinal liquor called haymaiden tea.

Hazen/hiessen – To forebode.

Head – To consult, conspire. *To zet ther heads together.*

Headland/hedlen – Ground or ridge under a hedge, at the heads of the ridge where the horses turn when ploughing.

Heal – To cover, hide. To heal beans is to earth up beans. *The house is unhealed* (The house is stripped, as by a rough wind).

Healen/hellen – Stones, flag-stones for roofing, whence hellier, a roofer.

Hean – The handle, as of a knife. *The knife's a-broke off up to the hean.*
Heft – Weight.
Helrut – The herb, Alexanders.
Herence – Hence.
Hereright – Here on the spot, at once.
Heth – The hearth, a heath.
Hethcropper – A pony bred on a heath.
Hick – To hop on one leg.
Hide – To whip.
Hiessen – To forebode evil. *It'll rain avore night*, says one. *There, don't be hiessenny*, answers another, who hopes it may not.
Highlows – A high shoe, lower than kitty boots.
Hike off/out – To go off hastily by compulsion, or actively to expel. *You shall hike out.*
Hile – Ten sheaves of corn set up in the field, four on each side and one at each end, forming a kind of roof.
Hipe – A heap.
Hippity-hoppity – Hopping.
Ho – Anxious care. *I don't know and don't ho* – I am not worried.

Hommicks

20

Hoils – The beard or awn of barley.

Hold wi' – To hold or side with, to follow in opinion. *To hold wi' the haire, an' run wit' the houns.*

Hollabaloo – noisy uproar.

Holm/ho'n – Holly, especially low and especially prickly holly.

Holrod – Cowslip.

Homble –Duck.

Home screech – Missel thrush.

Hommicks – Clumsy boots.

Honey-zuck – Honeysuckle.

Hook – To gore with the horns. A hooken bull is one that gores.

Hoop – Bullfinch.

Hornet – The common wasp.

Horridge/whorage – A house or nest of bad characters.

Ho's adder/hoss-tinger – Dragon fly.

Hoss-tongue – Hart's tongue.

Hounce – Hound or hunt out.

Hounds/bussels (of a waggon) – The slides or fellow-pieces.

Homble

21

Hountish – Doggish, nappish, snarling.
Howsh – A cry to swine, to stir them onwards.
Huckle – The hip.
Huckmuck – Wicker strainer put in a mashing tub to keep the grain from coming out with the wort.
Hud – The hull or legume of a plant.
Huddick/haddock – A bag or case for a sore finger.
Humbuz – A thin piece of wood with a notched edge which when swung round swiftly on a string makes a humming or buzzing sound.
Hummick – A heat or sweat.
Humstrum – A rude musical instrument.
Hungered – Hungry.
Hustle – To moan, spoken of the wind.
Hythe – A landing stead or haven where fish were landed.

I

Ice-candle – Icicle.
Iles (as ayels) - the awns as of barley.
Imma'bbee – It may be.

In jist – Almost, very nearly.
Inon – Onion.
Inon-rwope – Rope or string of onions.
Ire-gear – Iron ware.

J

Ja/jaw – A tenon for a mortise.
Jack-in-the-Green – Polyanthus.
Jack-o-lent – Scarecrow of old clothes, sometimes stuffed.
Jams – Wire shirt-buttons.
Janders – Jaundice.
Jib – A handbarrow, as a pig-jib for pig killing.
Jimmy – Door hinge.
Jist/jis' – Just, just about.
Jit – To jog, jut.
Jobbler/Underground jobbler – the wheatear.
Jut – To give a sudden blow or nudge.

Jack-o-lent

23

K

Keaf – Waste of short straws in threshing.
Keafen reake – A rake to clear the ceaf (chaff) from the corn.
Keakeham – Windpipe, particularly of slaughtered animal.
Keaple – The running socket in which a flail was
  fastened to the handstaff.
Kecks/kex – A stock of hemlock or cow parsley.
Kee – To tire out.
Keech – To cut grass and weeds in water.
Keeching-zive – A scythe for keeching.
Keepen – The burden or refrain of a song.
Keeve/kive – A large tub used for the wort to
  work in when brewing.
Kerf – The cut of a saw in wood.
Kerp – To talk mincingly.
Ketch – To set or harden, as melted fat.
Ketcher – The membrane over the viscera of a pig.
Keys – The seed vessels of the sycamore and maple.
Kid – A pod or legume, as a bean-kid, a pea-kid.

Kitty-coot

Killick rwope – The rope that fastens the killick stone to the boat.

Killick stwone – A stone used by fishermen as an anchor when fishing for pout etc.

Kind – Sleek, as of fur; also, keen as of a knife.

Kit – *All the whole kit o'm* means all the whole set, or tribe, of kindred.

Kitpat/kitbat – The clogged grease in the stocks of wheels.

Kitticoo – To push with one's elbows, as in getting through a crowd.

Kittyboots – A kind of short-laced boot, reaching up only over the ankles.

Kitty-coot – Water-rail.

Klink off – To go off as closely, or as unobserved as may be.

Knacker – A buyer of old out-worn horses for dog meat.

Knap – The unopened flower head of the potato and some other plants. *The teaties be out in knap.* Also, a small hillock, the brow of a hill.

Knee-knaps – Leathers worn over the knees by thatchers at work.

L

Lag – Leg.

Laggens – Leggings, short gaiters.

Lagwood – The bigger loppings of a tree.

Laminger – One became lame.

Lathy – Tall and thin.

Lauten-yeat – A great hurry.

Lawk – Look, behold.

Lawn/lawnd – Unploughed land, the unploughed part of an arable field. Also, a natural terrace on the sides of hills (a linch or linchet).

Leade – To dip up or draw off a liquid.

Leades – Raves of a wagon.

Leadecart – A cart with raves.

Leady's cushin – The thrift plant.

Lear – An ailing in sheep.

Lease – Glean.

Lease-carn – Corn gleaned.

Leat – To leak.

Leave – To lade out a liquid.

Lease/summerleaze – A field stocked through the summer as distinct from a mead which is mown; also ewelease, cowlease.

Ledgers – Rods that are fastened down by spars on the thatch of a rick or house.

Leer/leery/larry – Empty in the stomach, wanting food; or empty waggon.

Lentcorck – Crockery sherds, formerly thrown and smashed by boys on Shrove Tuesday.

Thomas Hardy's birthplace at Higher Bockhampton

Levers/livers/liver-leaves – The great yellow flag or its leaves.

Lew – Screened from the wind, lee. *In the lew zide o' the hedge.*

Lew/lew-warm – Luke-warm.

Lewth – Shelter from the wind. Warmth. *Come to the lew of the vire.*

Libbets – Rags in strips.

Lie – The lie of the country; the relative position of places. *I thought I codden be wrong, by the lie of the country.*

Ligget – Small bit of rag.

Limber – Very limp, flaccid.

Limbers – The shafts of a wagon.

Limmer – Painter, artist.

Linchet/linch – A ledge of ground on the side of a hill/the strip of green ground between two ledges.

Linded – A linded cow has a white streak down her back.

Line – To lean.

Linhay/linnedge – A low-roofed shed attached to a house, a penthouse.

Linnet – Lint, tinder.

Lin-man – A man in the flax-trade.

Lip – A vessel, a seed-lip, or seed-box, in which a sower carried his seed.

Lissen – A streak or layer, stratum. *There's a lissen o' bad hay in thik rick.*

Litsome/lissom – Of light and cheerful mind.

Litten – A long tale, a long noise.

Litty – Light and easy motion.

Loplolly – One who lops and lolls, a lazy or idle person.

'Lot or 'low – To allot or allow, to think or suppose. *'E do wish hizzuf out o't*, or *I do 'low*.

Lote/lo't (also lart) – A loft, the floor of an upper room, the ceiling.

Loup – A kind of sea louse, somewhat like a wood louse, which in warm summer weather eats the bait which fishermen set in lobster pots.

Lowsen – To listen.

Lug – A pole (land measure of five and a half yards).

Lumper – To stumble, tread loosely.

Lumpy – Heavy.

Lure – A disease of sheep; an ulcer in the cleft of the foot.

Lwoth – Loath, unwilling.

M

Madam – Used instead of Mrs as a remark of respect.

Madders/mathers – Stinking chamomile.

Made stone – Stone rough hewn at the quarry. To make stone means to hew it.
Magot – A whim or fancy.
Magoty – Fanciful, fond of experiments, crotchety.
Main – Mighty. *A main girt tree.*
Mainpin – Pin put through the fore-axle of a waggon for it to turn upon in locking.
Maintainance – Manure spread over land.
Mammet – An image, scarecrow.
Mandy – Saucy.
Man/maun – A maund, a large withy basket with two handles for apples, potatoes etc, in the shape of a cone.
Many – Much. *Do the cows gi'e many milk?*
Mark vor – To show tokens of becoming. *He do mark vor to be tall.*
Marten – A heifer that does not breed.
Mawken – A kind of mop for the oven.
Mazzerdy – Knotty.
Meaden – Same as madders.
Meal of milk – The milk of one milking.
Meary's tears – Spotted liverwort.

Meary's tears

Measoner – A mason.

Meat-weare – Food stuff.

Meech/mooch/mouch – To gather up things by picking, or begging.

Meesh – Moss; also, the run or lair of a hare.

Mel – To meddle.

Merry – The wild cherry.

Mid – May or might.

Miff – A slight mind-chafing with coolness between friends.

Miggy/muggy – A large white moth that flies at twilight.

Mind – To put in mind as well as to bear in mind. *Mind me o't tomorrow.*

Minnets – In marble play, knuckle down.

Mint – Mite.

Minty – Having mints (mites) in it, as rotten cheese.

Miz-mare – A mare.

Mock – The stump of a wride, as of hazel or other wood, or a tuft of sedgegrass.

Mommet – A guy, effigy.

Moot – The bottom of the stem of a felled tree, with its roots.

Merry

Mope/mwope – Bullfinch.
More – Tap-root of a plant.
Mote – Stem of grass.
Mouel – Field-mouse.
Mould – The top of the head or skull.
Mowburnt/mowbum'd – As corn or hay, burnt by heating in the mow or rick.

Muckle – Furze or heath laid in on the top of a drain before the earth was cast in.
Much – To smooth down, as a cat's hair.
Mullum – Soft and crumbling, as a mullum cheese.
Mummock – A fancy figure, an effigy, a guy.
Mump – One who is wont to beg of her neighbours.
Mutton-tops – Lamb's quarters. Also the young shoots of the goosefoot, sometimes boiled as a food-wort.
Mworish – So good as to wish to have more of it.

N

Naise – Noise. A scolding.
Nang/nangy – To mock by half-clear sounds, wagging

Mope/mwope

32

East Lulworth

the jaw with a grin. A great insult *enough to meake oone's blood bwile*.

Naps/knee-naps – Leathers worn over the knees by thatchers.

Nar – Never.

Near – Stingy, miserly.

Needs – Of necessity.

Nesseltripe – The most weakly or last of a brood of fowls, a fare of pigs, or a family of children.

O

O'Zundys – On Sundays.

Oben – Open.

Onlight – Alight, get off horse.

Ope – Opening in cliffs down to water side.

Organy – Plant of the mint tribe, marjoram/pennyroyal.

Orts – Leavings from hocks of hay on which cows are fed.

O's – Of us.

Out ov axen – Literally out of asking. Having had banns of marriage published three times.

Outstep – Out of the way, lonely – applied to village or house.

Overclap – Cloud. *Will it vreeze tonight? It will depend on the overclap.*
Oves/ovis – Eaves.
Overlook/auverlook – To look on with the evil eye.
Owl – To owl about, ramble by night.

𝒫

Pansherd – Potsherd.
Par – Confine, shut up; also surfeit.
Passel – Pencil.
Pa'sons an clarks – The running fiery spots on burning paper.
Peales – Railways.
Peane – Pane, as of glass or other flat surface.
Peart – Lively, quick, pert.
Peaviers – Paving stones, flagstones.

Passel

Peaze, peze – Ooze out, as water through some
  earthen vessels or from small openings. *The water
  pezed up vrom the ground at our he'th.*
Pelt – A fit of anger. *He went off in sich a pelt.*
Pewitt – Lapwing.

Pick – Hay-fork or dung fork.
Piers/pyers – Hand rails of a foot bridge.
Pill – Large brown pitcher.
Pillen/pelm – Dust.
Pim-sweale – Boil, pimple.
Pirty – Pretty.
Pirty deal – A great deal.
Pissabed – Dandelion, especially the narrow dandelion said to be very diuretic, hence its name.
Pitch – To put or throw up on a wagon; also to sit down.
Pitchers – Small square stones for pitching.
Pitchden pick – Long handled and long-pronged pick for putting up hay.
Plan – Middling. *Tis but a plan cup*. Also, quite. *The wind is plan south*. Also, homely, without affectation. *How d'ye like Mary? Oh very much. She is as plan as a dearymaid*. Also, unwell. *I be plan and poorly*.
Pleazer – Place.
Pleck – Small enclosure.
Plim – Swell.

Pissabed

Plounce – Plunge down as into water.

Pluffy – Plump, stout.

Pockfretten – Marked by smallpox.

Polly-wash-dish – Grey wagtail.

Pompen – Tea-kettle.

Pomper – To poke unskifully at a wound. *We had better not pomper 'en ourselves but call in a doctor.*

Pooch-pie – A pie made of a flat round of pastry doubled into a half circle, with fruit or meat within.

Pope – A baby, a doll.

Poppy – A dog.

Pounshall – Punctual.

Pride-o'-the'mamen – The foggy mist in the morning, likely to be followed by a warm day.

Promp – Prop.

Proof – Fattening quality.

Prove – Fatten, gain flesh.

Pummel-footed – Club-footed.

Pomster – Travel with a disease; not call in physician.

Punch – Pout.

Pompen

Pusky – Bloated.

A-put-out – Made angry.

Put to trouble – To prosecute at law.

Puxy – Miry or boggy place, puddly.

Pyer/pyer and lug – A rude bridge over a ditch, consisting of a pole (lug) to walk on and a handrail (pyer).

Q

Quaddle – To make limp or flabby; shrivelled.

Quarrel – Window pane.

Quarter evil – Disease of sheep.

Quest/quist – Wood pigeon.

Quirk – To let out breath suddenly and strongly after holding it.

Quob – To quiver like jelly.

Quont – A boat pole, forked at the outer end and used by fishermen to push flat-bottomed boats through passages or channels to Chesil Beach.

Quot – Low in proportion to breadth.

R

Raft – To rouse one as when going to sleep or dying, or to raft a beast. *Teake keare. The cow's arafted. Teake ceare; she mid hook ye.*

Rafty – Rancid, as 'rafty beacon'.

Rake – To reek.

Ram – Ramish, strong smelling, rank.

Rammil – Raw milk. Applied to cheese made of raw unskimmed milk.

Ramasens – Broad-leaved garlic.

Ram's claws – The stalks and stalk-roots of the creeping crow-foot, which often caught in the teeth of the haymakers' rakes, and sometimes broke off one of them.

Rand/ran/run – A hank of string. A length of twine.

Randy – A merry-making, an uproar.

Rangle – To reach about like trailing or climbing plants.

Rappen – Out-reaching, big.

Ratch – To stretch.

Rate – To scold, to accuse.

Rathe – Soon, early. Rathripe is an early apple.

Rather – Lately; just now. *He's rather a-come.*

Ratheripe – Early ripe (of fruit)

The verger, St Ann's Radipole, 1929

Rawn/rean – To raven or reach for food eagerly.

Ray – To array, put on raiment; to dress.

Rayen-zieve – A sieve, used chiefly in cleansing clover.

Read – The fourth stomach of ruminant animals.

Reake/reaky – *To reake a'ter plough* means to rake after the loaded hay-wagon.

Reames – A skeleton; the frame or ligaments of a thing.

Reamy – Something that may be pulled out without breaking, like hot toasted cheese. Spoken of slack bread.

Rear – To raise, to rouse, to excite. *You'll rear the weather* was said to one who, for a wonder, came to help in the hayfield.

Rearage – The number of sheep reared on a farm in one year.

Reddick/reddock/ruddock – Robin-redbreast.

Redeship – Reasoning, or ground of good reasoning. *You've a-put the knives across. We shall quarrel. Ah! there idden much redeship in that.*

Redroughs – Scarlet runners (french beans).

Redweed – Poppy.

Reef – A broad-reaching piece. *They've a-moved sich a reef o' groun' today.*

Reelly – To dance reels.

Reem – To stretch out, broaden, or lengthen.

Reer – Rare, underdone (of meat).

Reeve – To unravel, as a piece of knitting.

Renge – A hair sieve for flour or liquor.

Reremouse – Bat.

Rice – Brushwood.

Rick – A stack or mow with a sharp ridge or a pointed top.

Rid out a hedge – To clear unnecessary wood in laying of a hedge.

Ride – To be angry when teased or jeered. *I meade en ride.*

Rig – To climb or roam about.

Riggy/riggish – Sour.

Rile – To reach about as a restless child.

Redroughs

The Tudor Farm at Osmington, c1930

Rimer – A reamer. A tool for enlarging holes in metal.

Rine – Rind.

Ringle – Small ringing sound. *I heard the glass ringle when the winder wer a-broke.*

Rise – To raise, to get.

Rive – A rank smell, as that of a fox or badger.

Reremouse

Rivelled/rifled – Shrivelled as grass.

Roach – Rough, coarse, rank.

Robinhood – The red campion and the ragged robin.

Roll-er – A roll of wool. Hand carded wool was rolled off the cards in a little roll called a roll-er from the weakness of which came the saying *I'm so weak as a roll-er*. The 'o' in roll-er had the sound of 'o' in collar.

Rong – A rung, meaning also a cudgel or walking staff. Rundle or step of a ladder.

Rosom – A saw or proverb.

Rottlepenny – The yellow rattle.

Rottletraps – Rickety old household goods, etc.

Rouets – Tufts of rough grass.

Roughleaf – A true leaf of a plant, as distinct from its seed leaves or cotyledons.
Rout – A rut.
Rowse – To drive off, scare away. *Rowse the vowls out o' gearden.* Also, a noise.
  The bees be good when they do meake a rowse.
Rudder/rudern-sieve – A sieve for cleaning wheat.
Ruddle – A red earth by which they mark sheep.
Ruf – Roof.
Ruggle/ruckle – To rock or roll about. Also, to wheel as a barrow.
Rundlewood/randlewood – The small sticks from the head of a tree ripped of bark.

S

Sammel – A gutty, sandy earth mingled with soft stuff.
Sammel/sammy – A silly, simple fellow.
Sar – To serve or feed animals.
Sarch – Search; also, a fine hair sieve for meal.
Sassy – Saucy.
Sa't/sate – Soft.
Sa'tpoll – Soft poll, soft head, silly one.
Say – A slight trial. *Oone say, two say, dree and away,* the say being a slight movement

or running.

Scammish – Awkward, scram.

Scoop/scoopens – Scope.

Scote – To shoot along very fast, as in running.

Scrag – A very crooked branch of a tree.

Scraggy – Having many scrags.

Scraggle – To walk with the legs and body very crooked.

Scram – Screwy grown, dwarfish.

Scrape – A sheep-scrape, a bare place, where the turf has been scraped off by sheep's feet on a steep downside.

Screed – To shun, eschew.

Screak – To creak loudly.

Scriddick – A small scrap or shred.

Scrimpy – Scrimp-like, screwy, shrivelled, as half-starved.

Scrip – A hedger's or shepherd's coat, sometimes made of leather.

Scroff – Small bits of dead wood fallen under trees, or leavings under piles.

Scroop/scroopy – To give a low sound as of a hard surface scraping on another hard surface. If it is a shrill sound it is a creaking; if shrill and very strong, a screaking; if low, it is a scrooping.

Scrouge/scrush – To screw or squeeze up.

The Dairy House at Bloxworth, c1906

Scrounch/scrunch – To crunch strongly. *The dog do scrunch the bwone.*

Scud – A short slight shower cast from a flying cloud, a passing shower.

Scuff – To shove the foot along the floor or ground, like one slip-shod.

Scuff of the neck – The bare part of the neck close below the hair, and sometimes called the scruff of the neck.

Scute – A reward, pay.

Scwoce – To barter or exchange.

Seave the hay – *To seave the ha wi' the maidens*, is to cover them over with hay in play.

Seem an I – Seems to me.

Sess/siss – An exhortation to a dog to set him on somebody, or something.

Setty – Eggs on which the hen has sat for some while.

Shab off – To go off softly as if ashamed.

Shacklen – Loose limbed, lazy, as if shackle-boned, shaking about.

Shake – A crack in timber.

Shale – To take off the shell.

Shandy – As a bough that shies back from the stroke of the hook.

Shard – A broken piece, or a breach.

Shark/shirk off – To sneak off softly, from shame or an apprehension of danger.

Sharps – The shafts of a cart or other carriage. Also, a fine kind of bran.

Shatten – Shall not.

Shatter – To shed about in small quantities, as of hay or other loose stuff.

Shear – A ploughshare. Also, a crop of grass.

Sheen – To shame.

Shepherdess – The yellow wagtail.

Sheeted – A sheeted cow is one having a white band, like a sheet round its body.

Shirk – To sheer off, shun.

Shockle – To shake about, as marbles in a boy's pocket, or ripe seeds in a dry capsule.

Shod – To shed.

Shon't – Shall not.

Shook – Split, as wood by shrinking.

Shoot – Steep hill, or the road down it.

Sholduerens – Cider from shoulderings means from stolen apples carried home on the shoulders.

Shotten – Shall not.

Shove – A rough rolling of the sea.

Showl – A shovel.

Showance – Something to show as a proof, such as a written note.

Shram – A screwing up or out of the body and limbs from keen cold.

Shrimpy – Thin, arid, poor. Applied to land.

Shrocrop – The shrewmouse.

Shroud – To lop or prune the heads (shrouds) of timber trees.

Shrouded – Shrunk or curled up, as newly set plants, by heat.

Shrovy – *To goo a-shroven* was to go begging at Shrovetide. Also poor, mean as applied to land.

Shut – To join, as to weld two pieces of iron, or connect two pieces of wood. Also to agree. *We two can't shut*. Also to shut back, push back, as a cart by the horse.

Shut back – Shoot or push back. Spoken to a horse.

Sify – To catch the breath in sighing, to sob.

Sight – *Sich a sight o' vok*, or anything else, means such a number or quantity.

Silgreen – Houseleek.

Sippet – A little sop.

Sith – To sigh.

Sive – Scythe.

Sives – Chives; garlic used as a potherb.

Skicer – A lamb that runs too much.

Skiddle – To cut up wastefully.

Skiff – Askew, awkward (as left-handed); skiff-handed means having a distorted hand.

Skillen – A penthouse, shed.

Skilly – Scaly, niggardly.

Skim/skimmy – To mow the bunches of rank grass in a summerleaze.

Skit – To run or walk lightly, to shoot on.

Skiver – Skewer, a shaving or shiver of wood.

Skiver-wood – Spindle-tree, from which skewers were made.

Skurrick/skurrock – Small share. *Every skurrick o't* means every bit of it.

Slack-twisted – Inactive, lazy. Applied to a person.

Slait/slade – A sheepslait, a sheep-plain or down, a sheepleaze.

Slat – Slate. Also, the young and as yet flat pod as of the pea. Also to fling down carelessly. Also kidding or podding, as peas.

Slatch – To slake, to make slack, as lime by water.

Slent – To tear as linen. Also a slit.

Sleepy – Very loose or slack, as a rotten apple.

Slim – Slender. Also sly, scowling.

Slingers – Fir cones.

Skiver-wood

Slip – A cord or chain, to fasten a cow's neck to the tying in a stall.

Slips – Young weaned pigs running loose. Those somewhat older are hard slips; and others nearly full-grown are store pigs.

Slommock – Slatternly woman.

Slommocken – Dirty, or slatternly.

Sloo – Sloe.

Sloo (of a horn) – Inner bony prominence of a cow's horn.

Slooworm – Slow-worm, blind-worm.

Sluck-a-bed – A sluggard.

Slips

Smame – To smear.

Smatch – A taste, a smack.

Smatter – A mess.

Smeech/smeitch – Cloud of dust.

Smock-frock – A man's round frock of linen.

Smoor – To smear.

Snabble – To snap up hastily or greedily.

Snag – The small variety or species of sloe.

Snakeflower – The windflower, anemone nemorosa.

Snap – A small taking of food.

Snape – Spring.

Snapy – Springy, wet. Said of land.

Snappish – Wont to snap or snub off another's talk; short, angry answers.

Snead – The pole of a scythe.

Sniggle – To snort a little. Also to cut in small nicks or notches.

Snipe – The nose or peak of a boy's cap.

Snoatch – To speak or breathe hardly through the nose.

Snock – A smart knock; a short sound of a sudden blow.

Snoff –A candle-snuff. Also the eye of an apple.

Snorter/snatter – The wheatear bird.

Snotch – Wide notch.

Snout – To snub or snap off a speaker in a gruff tone.

Snoutish – Wont to snout.

Sog – To soak or loosen with wet. Spoken of land, or a road.

Sojer – Soldier.

Somewhen – At some time.

Soonere – Ghost.

So's – Souls.

So't – Soft.

So'tpoll – Poll (head), hence poll-tax, capitation tax. A pollard is a beheaded tree. Also a silly person.

Sowel/sole – A sharp shore or stake, such as is driven into ground to fasten up hurdles.

Span-new – Quite new, wholly new.

Sparbills – A kind of nail used in shoes.

Spargards – Gads, or sticks, to be split up into spars.

Spars – Sharp sticks, usually of withy or hazel, for fastening down thatch.

Spawl – A splinter flown off, as from stone.

Speaker – A long shoulder stake on which to carry a nitch of wood.

Spearde – Spade.

Speare – Thin.

Spet – Spit.

Spik/spike – Lavender.

Spiles – The beard of barley.

Spindle out – Spoken of young corn-plants which have begun to grow into stalks.

Spine – The coming turf of ground lately sown down to grass.

Spirt – To sprout, to vegetate.

Spitish – Spiteful, snappish.

George III Rewarding the Industrious Haymaker near Upwey, 1798

Spitter – Dock-spitters and thistle-spitters are tools to cut up docks or thistles.

Spleenish – Wild, headlong, hence a spleenish chap.

Sprack – Lively, springy, active.

Sprethe – To chap. *My lips be a-sprethed*.

Spry – Strong of muscle and springy.

Spuddle – To look for left-over potatoes.

Spudgel – A hollow kind of shovel for baling out water. Also to bale.

Squot – To flatten as by a blow, or make very quot.

Staddle – A wooden framework, or a bed of boughs, built to raise a rick off the ground.

Staddlen/staddling – Stuff to make a staddle.

Stairvoot – The bottom of the stairs.

Stan'by – To stand by one's word.

Stan'to – To *stan' to a chile* is to be sponsor.

To *stan' to an assertion* is to insist on it.

Stare – Starling.

Starry – Story.

Stean – To pave or furnish with stones. *A good steaned road.*

Steart – A sharp point, a tail. Hence the red-start, a bird with a red-tail.

Steer – Stir, uproar.

Stem – The handle of a pick or rake. Also, a stretch of time. To stemmy is to work or take on in turns, or stems, with another, to take one's turn.

Stick – A tree was often called a stick.

Stickland – Steep lane.

Stickle – Steep. *Theos hill is rather stickle.*

Stick's-end – The unburnt end of a stick from the fire.

Stitch – A set of sheaves stuck up in the field, top to top.

Stiver – To stiffen up much as an angry dog's hairs.

Stomachy – High-minded when insulted.

Stools – The roots of copse or hedgewood cut down nearly to the ground.

Stoor – To stir, as liquid.

Stout – The cowfly.

Stramote – A stalk of grass.

Strappen – Of great size.

Strapper – A helping labourer hired only for a busy time.

Stratch – Stretch. *An hour upon stretch.*

Stratcher/spreader – A stick to keep out the traces from the horses' legs.

Stubberd – An early kind of apple.

Stud – A steadfast stillness as of one in thought.

Stump – To become stiff or sturdy or sulky.

Stunpoll/stonehead/stunhead – Blockhead. Also an old, half-dead tree.

Suent – Smooth and even.

Sumple – Supple.

Swanskin – A very thick and close woollen cloth or flannel.

Sweal/zwel – To scorch.

Sweem/zwim – Giddiness. Formerly it meant a swooning. *My head do zwim.*

Swift – A wheel for spinning of hemp

Swipe – Very thin beer.

Swop – A strong whop (blow).

Tack – A shelf.

Trendle

Taffet – Dainty or nice food.

Taffle – To tangle, as grass or corn beaten down by the weather.

Thirtover/Thwart over – Perverse.

Three-cunnen – Over-sharp.

Tilt Bonnet – A garden bonnet without stuffing.

Timmersome – Restless, spoken of a child.

Tine – To hedge in ground/enclose with a fence; also to kindle a fire/candle.

Tip/Tuck a rick – Loose hay from the sides of the rick was used for tipping it.

Tiss/tess – To hiss strongly, as a cat, or as water cast on red hot iron.

Tistytosty – A child's toss ball of cowslips.

Tittery – Unstable, rather tottery or shaky.

Toleboy – Decoy.

Tooty – To cry, making a low, broken sound.

Trant – Originally a treading of the ground or road, tramping.

Tranter – A common carrier.

Trendle – Shallow tub.

Trimmen/trimmer – Great of its kind. *A trimmen crop o' grass. A trimmen girt heare.*

Trip – Culvert over a ditch or small watercourse. Also a fare (troop) of young pigs or a set of goslings.

Tuck out – To eat over-indulgently.

Tump – Hump or toft; a very small hillock or mound.

Tup – Young ram.

Tut – To do work by the tut is by the piece or lump, not by the day.

Tutt – Nosegay, a bunch of flowers.

Twiddick – Small twig.

Twin – A twain, two. Dorset speech says *John and Joe be a twin,* not twins (twains) which must be at least four.

Twink – Chaffinch.

Twiripe – Partly ripe.

Twite – To reproach, to twit.

Twoad/toad – A poor twoad is a wording of pity for one naked or helpless.

U

Undergroun' jobbler – Wheatear.

Unercheepen – Underhand.

Unray – Undress.

Uppen-stock – Mounting block.

Upsides wi' – Even with, having given another tit for tat.

Urge – Retch.

Use money – Interest on money.

V

Vang – To take, get, earn.
Vande – Farthing.
Veag – Wrath, high heat of anger.

W

Wagwanton – Quaking grass.
Ware – A sheep walk.
Waxen crundels/kernels – Enlarged tonsils, neck glands.
Wease – A crown put on head to take milk pail.
Weave – To rock back and forth as if in pain.
Whindle – Small and weakly, of a child or plant.
Whiver – To hover, quiver.
Whog – Go off to right (as spoken to a horse).
Whop – Blow from a strongly swung arm.
Wont-hill – Mole hill.

Wagwanton

Wops – Wasp.

Wornail/wornil – The larva of the cowfly growing under the skin of cattle.

Worret – To worry in small matters, tease.

Wrag – To scold, to accuse with bitter words.

Wride – A bush of many stems from one root.

Writh – The bond of a faggot.

Wrout – To grub up, as pigs do the ground.

Y

Yean – To lamb (spoken of a ewe)

Yeat-smasher – Wheatear.

Yoller/yollow wops – Yellow wasp.

Yop – Yelp.

Z

Za zaw – To saw.

Zebm/zeem – Seven.

Zedgemock – Tuft or bunch of sedge grass.

Yeat-smasher, also Undergroun' jobbler

Zeedlip – Seed box in which sower carried the seed.

Zee'd – Saw. *I zee'd you!*

Zet off/zet out – To start.

Zidelan – Slanting, sloping.

Zight – *Sich a zight o' vok*, or anything else, means such a number or quantity.

Zillgreen/silgreen – House leek.

Zive – Scythe.

Zog – Sog, soak, sink.

Harvesting at Sturminster Marshall

A passel of trades

BREWING

The *yoating vat* or *yoting stone* was a stone cistern formerly used in Dorset, as elsewhere, in brewing. When the beer or ale of a barrel had been drawn off down to the lowest tap, what was left below could not flow out but by the *heeling* (hanging over) of the barrel, which was called the *heeltap*. In Dorset *hele* or *heel*, as in *Shall I hele ye out* (pour you out) *a glass of eale?* originally meant to tip the jug.

FISHING

A *quont* was a stout pole forked at the top end and used by fishermen to push their flat-bottomed boats through passages or channels to Chesil Beach.

HARVEST-TIDE

Labourers in some parts of Dorset would say that at harvest time they required seven meals a day – *dewbit*, breakfast, luncheon, *cruncheon, nammit, crammit* and supper. According to Barnes, this seems to have been more a quaint jingle than an enumeration of meals, as some, eg *nammit* and *crammit*, appear to be one and the same.

Thatching

HAYMEAKEN

Haymaking formerly consisted of several operations which, with fine weather, followed each other thus: The mown grass – in *zwath, swath* – was thrown about – *tedded* – and afterwards turned once or twice. In the evening it was raked up into little ridges – *rollers* – single or double, as they might be formed by one raker, or by two raking against each other, and sometimes put up into small cones or heaps, called *cocks*. On the next morning the *rollers* or *cocks* were thrown about in *passels* (parcels), which, after being turned, were in the evening put up into *weales* (large ridges), the *weales* sometimes being *pooked* (put up into large cones – *pooks*) in which the hay was loaded. In raking grass into double *rollers*, or pushing hay up into *weales*, the *pickman* (fore-raker) was said to take in or push in – *row* or *roo* – and the other to close.

HAYWARD

A warden of the fences, or of a common, whose duty it was to see that it was not stocked by those who had no right of common, was known as a *hayward*. He sometimes *drove the common*, that is he drove all the stock into a corner and pounded such as were not owned by those who had a right of common.

HEDGE-CUTTING

To *trim* a hedge was to cut it into a good shape, while to *shear* a hedge meant to shear off unsightly outgrowth, though without aiming at neatness. A man who had begun to cut a hedge was aked if he was going to trim it. His answer was, *'No, only to shear 'en'*.

HOBBLE

An open field-shed for cattle was a *hobble*. The word also meant to tie an animal's legs

The Hangman's Cottage, Dorchester

to keep it from straying. The *hobble* was an instrument to confine the legs of a horse while it underwent an operation. Another meaning of *hobble* was a coarse laugh.

HOSS/HO'S

Apart from the meaning horse, this word was also applied to a plank or faggot to stand upon when digging in wet ditches. It was moved forwards by a knobbed stick put through it. *Not to hitch oon's horses together* meant not to agree or coincide in an opinion. In a team of horses, the shaft-horse or wheel-horse was called a *thriller* (from the Anglo-Saxon *thrill* – a shaft or pole); the horse next in front of him was the *boddy-hoss*, being by the waggoner's body. The next forward was the *lash-horse* being within reach of his lash while keeping by the side of the *boddy-horse*, and the fourth would be a *vollier*, or fore-hoss.

KNACKER

A *knacker* is defined in the Dorset Glossary as a buyer of old out-worn horses for dogs' meat. A *knacker* was also given as a collar-maker for horses, and Knacker's-hole, near Okeford Fitzpaine, might have been a lonesome spot fit for the *knacker's* work of putting a poor old horse for ever out of harness.

REAPING

There were three known ways of cutting wheat – *reapen* (reaping), *hewen* (hewing, believed to have been called *youghing* in West Dorset) and *hamen* (haming). Reaping consisted of the cutting of a handful of wheat at a time by drawing the sickle through it. In hewing, the wheat was probably chopped back against the standing corn, sufficient to make a sheaf. Haming was the cutting and taking back against the leg (protected by a strip of wood) of enough corn for a sheaf.

SPINNING

The spinning wheel with its appendages was known as a *turn*, and used to be seen in most cottages in Blackmore. The *turn* stood on a four-legged *tressel*, the wheel at the near end being 2-3ft wide. If the yarn was going up to the spool too finely, the spinner stepped forward to give it more wool, if it was too thick, she stepped back to give it less, so that she seemed to be executing a sort of dance.

TRIM

To keep oone in trim is to keep one in correct behaviour, or in a good state. Thus to *trim* a boat is to balance it or set it in a right position. Also, to *trim* a hedge is to cut it into good shape or state. To *shear* a hedge is to *shear* off ungainly or harmsome outgrowth without any main aim of trimness in the hedge.

WEAVING

So thick as inkle weavers. The word *thick*, as well as meaning that, also meant (as it still does) close in friendship. The *inkle* was a kind of tape which, with the weavers sitting side by side in close proximity, would call for a very narrow loom.

WOOLCOMBER

The trade of *woolcomber* was often found in the old jury lists of Blackmore men. The wool was combed, or carded, by two cards (*keards*) with square backs like brush backs and with handles, but faced with wire instead of bristles, the wool being pulled for a while between the cards, and then rolled off in *rollers*. A tale was told of an idle wife in Blackmore, who took in wool to card, and after a lengthy time, she had carded only two or three *rollers*. Fearing a scolding from her husband who believed in witchcraft, she aroused him in the night with the words, *'Oh, I've ahad twice the seame dream that my rollers have all been bewitched back again into loose wool. I'm sure it must be true. Do now step down an' zee.'* John did so, and came back with, *''Tis true enough. The rollers be out again in loose wool all but two or dree, an' they be so slack that they'll soon volly the rest.'*

Old Dorset sayings

A good steaned road — Paved or furnished with stones.

A hooken bull — A bull that gores.

A main girt tree — A mighty or very great tree.

A mampus o volk — A great number, a crowd.

An there I were all joppety-juppety — To express nervous trepidation caused by being flurried.

A pirty set-out — A pretty proceeding/start.

Aunt left her zome money an she were to live on the use money ot till she were 21. — Aunt left her some money and she was to live on the interest until she was 21.

By long an by leate — After a long time and much ado.

Can ye lend me a squinch o' tea? — Can you lend me a pinch of tea?

Cassen zee as well as cous cas? — Said to someone who had acquired his first spectacles.

Come, play Jonnik noo shufflen! — Be honest/fair/straightforward (west, north and south-east Dorset). In Purbeck, *jonick* had the meaning, jolly.

Come solid, goo sassy	Come solid, go saucy.
Don't go aniste/anewst 'en	Don't go near him.
Don't hearken to her trot	Don't listen to her foolish talk.
Don't loppy about, goo an' do zome at.	Don't lounge about lazily and idly.
Do ye pitch yourzelf in a chair	Do sit down!
Everyone do live to put a patch on their own children	Everyone lives to shield/cloak their own children.
Every jack-rag o'm	Every single individual.
For weetshoed thei gone	Wetshod.
Gie me my chipm/chipen brimmer	Give me my straw (or chip) hat.
Gi'es a pud	Give us a hand.
Good for the bider, bad vor the rider	Remunerative for the inhabitant, but inconvenient to travellers.
He an' I don't gee!	He and I don't get on!
He can preach well but don't goo by it	He can preach well but doesn't live by it.
He do mark vor to be tall	He shows signs of becoming tall.
He do ment his brother	He resembles his brother.
He had it all han'pat	He had it all at his finger ends.
Here be the reames of a bird	Here is a bird's skeleton.
He took off the church	He made a drawing of the church.

He went off in such a pelt	He went off in a fit of anger.
He were zoo azet up a-bout it	He was too upset about it.
He's a put-to vor money	He's in a strait.
He's a very speare man	He's very thin.
He's quite dunch	He's quite deaf/dull.
He's the very daps of his father	He's just like his father.
How b'ye? Pure, thank ye!	How are you? Quite well, thank you.
How flip e were!	How very kindly (or friendly) in talking.
How grete they two be!	How very friendly those two are!
How he's avell away/a-pitched away	How thin he's become.
How is heair do pout	How his hair pokes out (East Dorset).
How scram he do handle it	How awkwardly he handles it.
How the hoss do rawn in the hay	How the horse reaches eagerly for food.
How the ho'sses heair do stear	How stiff the horse's hair stands.
I can hardly wag	I can hardly stir.
I can't do it today beens I must go to town	I can't do it today as I must go to town.
I heard the cat squit droo the glass	Make a very slight sound.
I just gied en a touse in the head	A slight blow with the hand.
I never logged vrom school	I never played truant.
I should like to die awhole	Not in pieces, as in a railway smash.

I thank ye var the lence o't	I thank you for the loan of it.
I've a-hoppt my bwiler!	I've cracked my boiler.
I've a-rapped away the hoss	I've bartered/exchanged the horse.
I wer sweemish all day eesterday	Feeling a swimming in the head.
I'll gie thee a smamer!	I'll give you a good smack in the face.
I'll walk out to reem my lags	I'll go for a walk to stretch my legs.
Jeeminei/Good Jeminei	Oh brave! - a cry of wonder.
Lend me thy knife, woot?	Lend me your knife, will you?
L'ok zee	Look, see you.
Lwoth to bed, an lwoth to rise	Said of sluggards.
Mether Ho!Come hither ho!	A carter's call to a horse when driving.
Mind, you'll stab the wrack o't	You will have to stand (take) the consequences.
Nar brick nor brack	Of a perfect item – unflawed.
Noo girt sheakes	No great things – nothing to brag about.
Shall I hele out another cup?	Shall I pour out another cup?
She do look solid	She looks serious/gentle.
She's always in a fantod about Meary	She's always in a fuss/fidget about Mary.
She's always a trapesen about	She's always tramping around.

73

She were in such a tilt	She was so angry.
She's quite dark	She's quite blind.
That cloth is so thin's a wevvet	That cloth is as thin as a cobweb.
That wheat is lavish	That wheat is rank.
That's a fine stick!	That's a fine tree!
The mead were hained/winterhained	The field was laid up/not stocked.
The vrost do gi'e	The frost yields or thaws.
The vu'st bird, the vu'st cass	The first bird, the first earthworm.
The young birds be nearly flushed	The young birds be nearly fledged.
There, dont be hiessenny	Don't forebode evil.
There's a fess feller!	There's a fussy/meddling fellow.
There's a hedlen chile!	There's a headlong/giddy child!
There's a little quot rick	There's a hayrick low in proportion to its breadth.
There's a turk of a rat!	A big or formidable one.
This beacon do plim in bwilen	This bacon swells when boiled.
This day ze'nni't	Today week.
This meat is nesh!	This meat is tender.
This is a miz job!	This is a mis-happening.
Tis a very lippy/lippen time	The weather is very rainy/stormy.

To zet their heads together   To consult, conspire.
Well, we mus' put up wi' it   Well, we must put up with it (the
       weather) without any bad feeling.

We shall ha' rain; the stwones do eve   We shall have rain; the stones are damp.
We've hardly keep enough   We've hardly enough food for the cattle.
What a magoty man he is!   What a fanciful/crotchety man!
What a pwop/pope of a thing!   What a big puppet! – a term of reproach.
You be a soggy young chap!   You are heavy to lift!
You fin(n)eged!   You didnt answer the call of duty!
You'll dreve me torrididdle   You'll drive me almost mad!
Zit down! A riggen about zoo   Sit down! You're roaming about so!

Dialect greats

William Barnes, undoubtedly the most outstanding of Dorset's dialect speakers and writers, was born in 1801 at Pentridge in the north-east of the county. His father, a farmer, moved soon after to Bagber Common, and the young Barnes attended the national school at nearby Sturminster Newton. He left school at the age of thirteen, the schoolmaster describing him as 'his brightest pupil'. Being of a studious turn of mind, he was able to educate himself further and to take up teaching at the age of twenty-three. He taught at Mere in Wiltshire for twelve years where he met and married his wife Julia. Later he ran a school in Dorchester. After taking a ten-year part-time degree course in divinity Barnes was ordained into the Church of England. He became rector, for five years, of Whitcombe, and later of Winterborne Came, both churches being approximately three miles outside Dorchester.

Barnes was familiar with more than sixty languages, he was a musician, artist and playwright, and wrote knowledgeably on a number of subjects, including archaeology. He was best known, however, for his poems in the Dorset dialect; many have since been translated into standard English.

In addition to studying languages, publishing school books and a book on the English tongue, Barnes had started writing in what he called the 'language of King Alfred' while at Mere. Here are some examples of his many poems:

PRAISE O' DO'SET

> *If you in Dorset be a-roamen,*
> *An ha' business at a farm,*
> *Then woont ye zee your eale a-foamen,*
> *Or your cider down to warm!*
> *Woont ye have brown bread a-put ye,*
> *Butter? – rolls o't,*
> *Cream – why bowls o't,*

Woont ye have, in short, your vill,
A-gi'ed wi' a right good will!

(Chorus)
Friend an' wife,
Fathers, mothers, sisters, brothers,
Happy, happy, be their life!
Vor Dorset dear
Then gi'e woone cheer,
D'ye hear? Woone cheer!

BE'MI'STER (BEAMINSTER)

Sweet Be'mi'ster, that bist a-bound
By green an' woody hills all round,
Wi' hedges, reachen up between
A thousan' vields o'zummer green ,
Where elems' lofty heads do drow
Their sheades vor hay-meakers below,

An' wild hedge-flow'rs do charm the souls
O' maidens in their evenen strolls.

Barnes also described, in the following couplet, the broad valley bounded by lofty downs on which stands Cerne Abbas:

The zwellin downs, wi' chalky tracks
Aclimmin up their zunny backs.

And of the feasting and dancing that took place on the village green at Bishop's Caundle after the Battle of Waterloo, he wrote:

In Caundle, vor a day at least,
You woudden vind a scowlen feace,
Or dumpy heart in all the pleace.

Another in nostalgic mood, written towards the end of his life, was his last poem. Perhaps when he wrote it he felt his end was near.

THE GEATE A-VALLEN TO

Zoo now I hope his kindly feace
Is gone to vind a better pleace,
But still wi' vo'k a-aeft behind,
He'll always be a 'kept in mind.
Vor Lydlinch bells be good vor spirit
And liked by all the neighbours round.

Barnes died at Came Rectory on October 7, 1886, and an imposing bronze statue to his memory stands outside St Peter's Church, Dorchester, where he appears as a dignified figure wearing a frock coat, knee breeches and buckled shoes.

Sadly, his poems in the Dorset dialect did not provide him with a living wage and brought him fame only after his death.

Now - a modern poet, E J 'Beau' Parke was born and brought up in Lytchett Matravers, Poole, and left after serving in the forces during the Second World War. He lived in London and regularly visited Lytchett, returning to live near his birthplace in 1986. His great- great- great- great-grandfather, John Parsons, was known as the Lytchett poet. The following poem is taken from Beau Parke's book of poems and short essays entitled *From the Lower Garden Gate*. It tells the story of the fire-watchers' log. Lytchett man George Wilson, who had initiated the log, and supervised it during the Second World War, went to Australia in the late 1950s with his twin sons. He took the log with him. George died in Australia and in the 1980s the twins returned to Dorset for a holiday. In Lytchett they met old acquaintances with whom they left the log, saying that Lytchett was a more appropriate home for it.

UPPER LYTCHETT'S FIRE-WATCHERS, 1940-43

I be one o' Georgie Wilson's eager vire-watchin' boys,
My yurs 're trained t'listen for that throbbin' engine noise
Of them gert big Jerry bombers who d' drop their zendaries
An' burn arr British 'omeland so's't' bring us to arr knees.

'Well we ain'ta goinna have it, not George Wilson's boys,
We'm goinna beat they Germans, wi' all their wicked ploys,
Arr stirrup pumps 're read, aar buckets and our zand,

We be probably the vinest vire'vighters in the land.

Another modern poet is Devina Symes, who lives in West Lulworth. She has been a William Barnes' enthusiast since reading his poems at the age of twelve. At the age of twelve she wrote her first poem in the Dorset dialect, following which many more of her poems appeared - and still do - in the Dorset Year Book.

DARZET VOLK

Zome think we Darzet volk be daft
'cause of the way we do zpeak
Well tidn't zo, we cin rad and write
And we do know the days of the week.

We do know inough to get we by
And not inough to make we depressed
We be 'appy volk, content wi' our lot

That's more than you can zay for the rest.
We 'ave nar reason to veel evil minded

In Darzet there be beauty all around
Livin yer do make ee veel good
No prettier place cin be vound.

No we bain't ashamed of what we be
We be honest volk be choice
We do live our lives for every day
We be proud of our Darzet voice.

Devina Symes has been a member of the William Barnes' Society since 1986 and has served on the Committee for the last three years.

Statue of William Barnes outside
St Peter's Church, Dorchester

A Dorset miscellany

Here are some of the games that Dorset children used to play, superstitions and saws, long-ago customs and traditions, and a few local eccentricities.

BARLEY-BREECH/BREACH. This was a game of catch played by six. The catchers stood in the middle on ground called 'hell'. William Barnes said that he saw it played with one catcher on hands and knees in the small ring (hell) with the others dancing round the ring crying:

> *Burn the wold witch you barley-breech*

DIBS. A game of toss and catch usually played by two children, with five knucklebones, a leg of mutton, or round pieces of tile or slate.

HIDY-BUCK was the name for a game of hide-and-seek.

KERNEL was a name commonly applied to the pips of pomaceous fruit, which were sometimes playfully shot from between the thumb and forefinger by young folks after chanting the following words:

> *Kernel, come, kernel! Hop over my thumb,*
> *And tell me which way my true-love will come;*
> *East, west, north, or south,*
> *Kernel, jump into my true-love's mouth.*

LAMPLOO was an outdoor game played by boys.

LET, meaning a stopping or interruption, was used by boys playing marbles. *'Let shall be,'* they would say, *'an accidental stopping shall be fair.'*

MAG was a mark or stake to throw at, as in quoits or pitch-half-penny. It was also the name of a game played by boys in which the players threw at a stone set up on edge.

MILLER/MILLARD was a large white moth that flew at twilight, such as the pale tussock-moth or the puss-moth. Children sometimes caught these moths and, after interrogating them on their taking of toll, made them plead guilty and condemned them in the following lines:

> *Millery, millery, dowsty poll,*
> *How many zacks hast thee a-stole?*
> *Vow'r an' twenty an' a peck,*
> *Hang the miller up by's neck.*

MUMMERS were young men who went round at Christmastide bedecked with ribbons and tinsel (one of them being Father Christmas), to act a little play which included a fight between a Turkish knight and King George of England.

NURSERY RHYME IN DIALECT

> *Laidy bird, laidy bird,*
> *Vlee away hwome,*
> *Our house is a-vire,*
> *Your children will burn.*

BARNABY BRIGHT — *The longest day an' the shortest night,* said of Barnabas-day, about the midsummer solstice.

MONEYSPIDER. When folk saw a moneyspider hanging from a thread they sometimes took and tried to swing it round their heads three times without throwing it off; then they put it into their pockets, whither it was believed it would soon bring money.

SHEEP. Dorset sheep, sometimes so called, are a fair, horned variety. It has been said of the Southdown sheep of Sussex and Dorset sheep:

> *Those (Southdowns) a finer wool may yield,*
> *But these (Dorset) are fairer in the field.*

AN EXHORTATION TO A DORSET MILLER. The following notice is to be seen on the picturesque mill at Fiddleford, a hamlet lying a mile or so down river from Sturminster Newton. All that remains of this medieval manor house, built *c*1380, are the two-storeyed wing and half the hall, restored in the 1960s by the then Ministry of Works. The strange inscription chiselled into the wall is dated 1566. It is well-worn and not easy to read.

> *He that wyll have anythinge done*
> *Let him com fryndly he shall be welcome:*
> *A frynd to the owner and enemy to no man.*
> *Pass all here freely to com when they can,*
> *For the tale of troth I do always professe;*
> *Myller be true; disgrace not thy vest*
> *I falsehod appeare the fault shall be thyne*
> *And of sharpe punishment think me not unkind…*
> *Therefore to be true it shall the behove*
> *(To) please god chefly (that liveth) above.*

HIC A'TER HOCK (OR HICKER TO HACKER). The pursued apparently pursuing the pursuer. If a dog were running round in a broad circle after a hare, and the hare was farther than half of the circle in front of the dog, he would appear to be the catcher. A man, telling of seeing such a case of hounds and hare, said, *'There they went hicker to hacker all auver, John's hounds avore and the heare a'ter'*.

A DORSET WISHING CHAPEL. In the village of Abbotsbury, on top of a steep 250ft hill grazed by hundreds of sheep, stands St Catherine's Chapel which for centuries acted as a look-out and beacon. St Catherine was the patron saint of spinsters and was supposed to be able to work miracles for them. A local couplet runs:

St Catherine, St. Catherine, lend me thine aid,
And grant that I never may die an old maid.

A verse on the same theme contains an element of urgency:

A husband, St Catherine
A good one, St Catherine
But 'arn a one better
Than narn a one Catherine.

And another states succinctly:

Sweet St Catherine,
A husband St Catherine

Rich, St Catherine,
Soon, St Catherine.

Whether the saint had any success is not known.

A BED CHARM

Matthew, Mark, Luke and John
Be blest the bed that I lie on
Vow'r corners to my bed
Vow'r angels all a-spread
Oone at head an' oone at veet
An' two to keep my soul asleep.

A DORSET CUSTOM. Dorset had its fair share of old customs, one of which was connected with the Isle of Portland and took place on November 5. A bonfire would be lit and at a given signal a man would take a child in his arms. Then all the other children would follow him in single file around the bonfire, over which he would eventually leap, still holding the child. As the fire began to burn low, the children would jump over it too, to the accompaniment of the following doggerel:

> *Wood and straw do burn likewise,*
> *Take care the blankers* (flying particles)
> *Don't dout* (put out) *your eyes.*

LARRENCE/LAWRENCE. For some cause which has not been discovered, Larrence (or Lawrence) was in some parts of Dorset the patron or personification of laziness. When someone was seen to be lazy, Lawrence was said to have him, and when one felt a loathing of work, he would sometimes cry:

> *Leazy Lawrence, let me goo!*
> *Don't hold me summer and winter too.*

SLUGGARD'S GUISE. On the same theme, a sluggard's guise meant a sluggard's manner, as in the following couplet:

> *Sluggard's guise,*
> *Lwoth to goo to bed, an' lwoth to rise.*

GIFTS. White spots on fingernails were believed to betoken coming presents.

Gifts I think, sure to come,
Gifts on the vinger, sure to linger.

SAYINGS. The following conversation might be construed differently today from how it was in times past:

'Why don't ye come to church, John?'
'Oh, Mr H is too high vor me.'

The word 'high' here was used to indicate that the sermons in question were 'high in hard words', ie of Latin and Greek, rendering them difficult to understand. A current saying of the time, quoted by William Barnes, was:

'It has been said of these folks' speech that everything is "he", except for a tom-cat which is termed a "she".'

DORSET SMUGGLERS. The village of Owermoigne lying off the road which runs between Dorchester and Wool was in past times the haunt of smugglers. There were those of an age to recall some of these events, but they preferred to veil their memories in phrases such as:

'What father did say…' or 'What granfer twold I!'

THE MILITARY PARADE AND THE UNWILLING PARTICIPANT. The lines below comprise the first verse of William Barnes' poem *Nanny Gill*. They refer to an event which took place during the Napoleonic wars, although there is another version of the story which features Old Grace (instead of Nanny Gill) and a donkey (instead of a horse).

Nanny Gill, a fisherwoman living at Abbotsbury, owned a horse which had once served with the military and of which she was very proud. On one occasion, she was transporting fish from Abbotsbury to Dorchester market, wearing a red cloak and black bonnet, when disaster occurred.

A review with mock fighting was taking place at Maiden Castle and, forgetting about her steed's erstwhile warlike connections, she pulled up to watch the proceedings. Horror of horrors – as the trumpets blew the charge, the former cavalry horse leapt forward and, regardless of its owner's frantic tuggings and pleadings, dashed off at top speed, the mackerel pots bumping on either side of him and Nan's cloak billowing out behind her.

As her horse lined up with the others, his embarrassed rider on his back, King George III, who had watched the event with great amusement, burst into loud laughter.

> *Ah! they wer times, when Nanny Gill*
> *Went so'jeren ageanst her will,*
> *Back when the King come down to view*
> *His ho'se an' voot, in red an' blue;*
> *An' they did march in rows,*
> *An' wheel in lines an' bows,*
> *Below the King's own nose;*
> *An' guns did pwoint, an' swords did gleare,*
> *A-fighten foes that werden there.*

WHERE ARE YOU TO? Dorset folk often say, *'Where do ye live to/bide to?'* and keep other old uses of 'to' as an adverb, as in *'Put to the hoss,' 'Shut to the door!'* Also, *'to year'* for 'this year', and *'to-day'* for 'this day'. Also, *'to'* for 'at', as in *'to whome'*, for 'at home'.

JARGE AN' 'IS DOG. *'T'other day I was gwine across a vield out Corfe Castle way, when I zeed Jarge wi' his dog looken ader zome sheep. I notic'd the dog was zetten down looken very mis'rable, meaken a whinen noise, zoo I zed, "Wot's the matter wi' yer dog, Jarge?". "There bain't nothen the matter wi' en," Jarge zed, "ee be on'y lazy, that's all." "But, Jarge," I zed, "zurely that cain't be right; laziness wou'den meake en carry on like that." "O ees twou'd," Jarge zed. "The vact is that there dog be a-zetten down on thistle, an' ee be too lazy t' git off o' it."*

THE SHAPWICK MONSTER. Shapwick is noted for an event – said to have taken place on October 12, 1706 – concerning a fisherman who was passing through the village when he dropped a large live crab from his basket. Much alarmed at the unaccustomed sight, the villagers hurried off to fetch, in a wheelbarrow, the oldest inhabitant, who roared in alarm:

''Tis a land monster, wheel me off!'

A DORSET EPITAPH. At the sixteenth century church at Bloxworth, outside the porch, is the tomb of Parson Welsteed. His epitaph begins:

Maypole, Sturminster Marshall

*Here lyes that revered orthodox devine
Grave Mr. Welsteed aged seventy-nine
He was the painfull pastor of this place,
Fifty five yeers compleete.'*

The word *'painfull'* is probably used in the old meaning of 'painstaking'.

DORSET FLOPPER. Coming up to date, this is a term usually used to describe a skittle player who ends up either on his/her knees or completely prone during the delivery of a ball down a skittle alley.

Some Dorset delicacies

SHERBORNE STODGER

Last baked about eighty years ago by a Mr Dewey at the Parade in Cheap Street, Sherborne, the confectionery known as the Sherborne Stodger was made from enriched bun dough, with dried fruit and spice. In those days, seven Stodgers cost 6d. However, they did not last very well, so by the second day they had to be toasted and were renamed – somewhat unappetisingly – Gutscrapers. The recipe has been rediscovered in recent years and is given in *Sherborne Camera* by Katherine Barker, so Sherborne Stodgers are available once again at the Three Wishes coffee shop and restaurant in Sherborne, at the increased price of £2, including a pot of tea for one.

DORSET APPLE CAKE

This Dorset speciality seems too well-known to be included in this chapter, yet it is too much a part of the county to be omitted. All true Dorset folk are familiar with the recipe, though the variations are numerous. None of the eighteenth century manuscript cookery books have it, but a very simple recipe from Marnhull, believed to date from the 1860s, was recorded in 1940. Here is a basic recipe for Dorset Apple Cake.

115g (8oz) butter
4 large eggs
25g cornflour
225g chopped bramley apples
225g caster sugar
250g self-raising flour
extra apple slices
lemon juice
soft brown sugar

Cream the butter and caster sugar together in a bowl. Add the eggs, flour and cornflour, and mix well. Fold the apples into the mixture and pour into a well-greased cake tin (18cm or 7in). To decorate the cake, cut unpeeled slices of apple and soak in lemon juice, then

Dorset Apple Cake

arrange in a circular pattern on top of the cake and dust with soft brown sugar to make a crusty glaze. Bake in the oven at 170C for about 75 minutes.

In the Dorset dialect, should you be *leary* (hungry) and in need of *nammet* (food), a meal of *nedlins* (pig's innards) – so I have read – followed by Dorset Apple Cake will put you to rights. Or you might prefer a succulent piece of *nesh* (meat).

Here is a selection of Dorset recipes from the seventeenth century.

BEEF TROMBTON

Take a peace of Flank of Beef according to your Dish, put it on the fire with as much watter as will cover it, Skin it Clean: Then add a dozen of Large Onions and Six Carrots, Three Parsnips four Turnips a little Cloves mace and hole Peper, and a bunch of Thyme parslees & Salary: Let all this stew for about five Hours very slow, Season it to your tast: Then serve it with the Sauce as Following, take some Thyme parsley and sweet herbs, Chop them small one Anchovie Chopt small, some capors Chopt small, put it in a Sauce Pann with some Culley or thick gravie: Set it over the fire to boil and serve it Up.

TRIPE PIES

Tak ye leanest trips you can get if they have bene sowst lay them a soak in bear if new in water and salt when they have layen 4 or 5 howers tak them out and dry them in a cloath when you have paired of ye ruff of both sids then mince them very small then put in som suet and som salt and som smale mace without beating a good deale a nutmegge smal beaten then chop it well together and afterwards put in your currants and when your pies be baked you must put in good store of sugar.

TO MAKE A HARTY CHOCK (ARTICHOKE) PIE

Take one dozen of ye bottoms of harty chockes that are not full ripe cut them and boile them to that porpose but not over tender then take a pint of whit wine three quarters of a pound of sugar large mase a good quantity on dozen of dates season ye bottomes with nutmegs and salte a little and a very little pepper put all these into a puter dish and let it stand on a chafing dish of coales and stue to howers then set it by being cloz covered when you put them into ye pie take ye bootoms from ye liquer with ye mace and dates and put to them good store of marrow and fresh butter for ye liquer put not that in till ye pie be hard which will be in half an hower and after ye liquer is in let it stand so much longer then take it for your use.

This recipe was devised *'For Weak Persons'*

2 oz isinglass
fi oz gum arabic
2 oz sugar candy
Half a small nutmeg grated
1 pint of port or sherry
Let it steep all night and then simmer till all the ingredients are dissolved. Strain it and when cold it will be a jelly.

ROAST MACKRILL

When yr Mackrill are open'd & wash't put a pudding in to their bellys made with mackrill Herbs and swet Herbs some Crumbs of Bread yelks of Eggs peper salt nitmeg and butter so make it up in a paist & sew it up in thire bellyes butter a Dripping Pan & Lay them in it before ye fire turning them as Occation requires baste them with butter & strew some salt on y:m: and some flower w:n they are allmost done enough strew some shrid herbs and Crumbs of bread on them you must make the sause with Gravey Clarett Anchovies onion peper salt and the pudding that was roasted in the mackrill some juce of Lemon and thicken it with butter.

MARCHPANE CAKES

Take 3 pennyworth of gumdragon (Tragacanth) lay it in Rose water all night putting more water to it if the first dry up, and the gum be not like jelly then take a lb of Almonds, 2 lbs of Sugar blanch the almonds out of hot water into cold a little while then take them out of that cold water & put them into more then put them into a mortar & beat them with as much gum as will lye on a shilling then put to it your sugar being pound very fine & sifted beat it well till it comes to a perfect past then take it out of the mortar & role it out about the thickness of a crown piece, cut it with a sack glass about the bigness of a crown piece then make them with a small edge, round them, & ice them with Candy icing, & strew them all over with couloured Carraway Comfigo. Set them in a warm oven or a stove to Dry if you please you may put into it a grain of ambergrease.

DORSET KNOBS

First baked in the mid-nineteenth century by Eleanor and Samuel Moores at their small bakery in the Marshwood Vale, Dorset Knob biscuits were a traditional start to the working day of every local farm labourer. The bakery moved to its present Morcombelake site in 1880 where it continued to turn out these delicious crunchy biscuits in their distinctive tins, and still does today.

BLUE VINNEY CHEESE

Vinny and vinnied meant veined – so Blue Vinney cheese was a blue veined cheese having the appearance of blue mould or fungus. Hence, blue mouldy Dorset cheese. It was traditionally made in Dorset from hand-skimmed milk leaving behind some cream. Rennet was added and the cheese turned for a while – a lengthy process which began to die out until recent years when it was revived.

Dorset Knobs and Blue Vinney cheese went well together and have always rounded off the annual dinner of the Society of Dorset Men, together with a poem in praise of the cheese.

Dorset Knobs and Blue Vinney Cheese

The Wishing Well at Upwey, c1900

'Neath the clavy, a Hardyland sketch

M rs. Podger was in excellent spirits – to use her own phrase, she felt 'proper vitty' – for had not her friend Mrs. Sapseed come all the way from Burmouth to see her? And Mrs. Sapseed had the enviable reputation of being able to talk faster than anyone in that corner of the county.

'Now do'ee zit down,' blustered Mrs. Podger, 'draw up closer to the vire, and let I warm zome zlippers, vur I be afeared the rain ha' zoaked droo thy booates.'

Mrs. Sapseed took off her wet boots, pulled on the proffered slippers, and the two settled themselves.

'We better teake care,' whispered Mrs. Podger, jerking her thumb towards the wall, 'the neighbour woman be a terrible listener, 'er be, and the walls be that thin 'er kin hear every word.'

Barely had the warning left her lips when the latch of the outer door clicked up, and a raucous voice from the far end of the passage cried cautiously: 'Mrs. Podger! – have'ee – excuse I makin' so bold – but have'ee got anybody there you don't want?'

Mrs. Sapseed started violently and looked perplexed at this strange and unexpected query from the unknown voice without, while Mrs. Podger hastened to reply: 'Lar no, Mrs. Gudge, but I've a-got zumbody here I do want, and who I'd like to kip here vur a month if 'er 'ud bide long wi' I.'

'I zeed zumbody a-comin' up thy garden path,' rejoined Mrs. Gudge by way of explanation, 'and I thought as 'ow you mid be up a'dressin', zo I comed in to zee if all was saff,' and out again went the old neighbour woman.

'Well,' commented Mrs. Podger when the intruder was well out of hearing, 'er comed in here vur one or t'other o' two things. 'Er either wanted to zee who I'd a-got here, or else 'er took you vur one o' they dicked-up thieves that we do hear about – them as do dress theirzelves up to look proper gentry-like and upperstolick, and be only thieves adder all. But doant'ee mind 'er, Mrs. Sapseed – doant'ee teake no notice; 'er do mean kind enough, and we be that plagued wi' the gipsies that do pitch on Canmere Common that 'er thought 'er 'ud gi' a look in, poor wold zoul!'

However much Mrs. Sapseed disliked being mistaken for a 'dicked-up thief,' she swallowed her indignation and astonishment. She had much to say, and had come over expressly to compare notes with Mrs. Podger. What they imparted to each other on these occasions furnished food for reflection for many future days.

'I were a-goin' to ask 'ee,' resumed Mrs. Podger, 'how that there Betty Leech is gittin' on – 'er as used to be dairymaid to Squire Lorridon yonder. 'Er went zomewhere up your way when 'er left here, didn't 'er?'

'Betty Leech!' exclaimed Mrs. Sapseed, 'why 'er's married. 'Er married 'igh too. Why, bless yer 'art, theed'st ought to zee her 'igh notions. The latest is 'ow 'er do goo in vur addernoon tay – zame as Vicar's lady.'

Mrs. Podger gasped, but before she could express her amazement the narrator continued: 'I went to her house t'other day, and 'er asked I in to addernoon tay. Zoon as I zot down Betty's mother up and zays, 'Now do'ee, Mrs. Sapseed, teaste zome o' Betty's pertater ceakes - 'er own meakin!!' - Mrs. Sapseed sniffed her contempt – 'Tiddy-ceakes vur addernoon tay – tiddy-ceakes! I thought as 'ow I'd teake a rise out o Betty, zoo I up and zaid, "Lar Betty, I bean't a-gooin' to bide where they do only gi' I tiddy-ceakes vur addernoon tay! Why can't 'ee 'ave sponge-ceakes, and zome rale chiny that I kin zee me hand droo when I come to zee'ee?" 'Er didn't like that, 'er didn't , and I hain't been there zince.'

Mrs. Sapseed was now like a hoop set a-trundle down a hill – she had started and didn't mean to stop. Her news, bottled up for many a week before, must now bubble out. Into the delighted ears of Mrs. Podger ran the kindly gossip and quaint scandal of the countyside, while she sat with undisguised admiration of her friend's 'powers o' spache.'

'An' now that do remind I – who do'ee think I runned into as I comed out o' Betty's? Thee coosen never guess, Mrs. Podger, zo I'll tell 'ee – why wold Sam'l Crabb, zame as used to bide 'long be Varmer Todd as carter. I hadn't zeed 'er vir nigh vifteen year, nor 'ee hadn't zeed I nuther. I ztared at 'ee, and 'ee stared at I, and then 'ee up and zays to I. "Why, 'tes you, idden it?" and I zys to 'ee, "Ees, and zo 'tes you idden it?" "Zure 'nuff 'tes," 'er zaid, "you wuz a Miss Snooks avore you marr'd warn't 'ee?" "I was zo," I zaid, "and where be you to now, Sam'l?" "I've a-lef' Middicombe," er zaid, "and I do live to Durton now." "Be married?" I as't 'en. "Ees, 'er zaid, "and I'll tell 'ee all about it." And this is what wold Sam'l told I, Mrs. Podger, 'er did.'

'"Maybe, thee cass mind that I were tarr'ble zweet on Hetty Fudge. I wanted 'er bad, but wold Jan Cood bested I 'er did – bested I and 'ad Hetty. I zeed 'er in market the week avore 'er were hitched. 'I do veel tarr'ble zad, Hetty,' I zaid, 'you'll zend I a bit o'bride-ceake, wont 'ee now?' 'No daz'ee! Thee shassn't have nar a bit,' zaid Hetty, proper sharplike. Well, 'er got marr'd, an' I dedn't get no ceake. You'll mind I kep' company wi' Annie Ray – a pleasant-spoken zort of a maid 'er wuz, but I soonest 'ave 'ad Hetty. Things turned out passin' strange. Poor Annie died, and just 'bout zame time I heard as 'ow wold Jan 'ad died too. Poor wold feller! …. Adder a time I thought as 'ow I'd better goo and look Hetty up, zoo I went up country one day. Proper nice liddle varm 'er 'ad up there, and I zeed Hetty a-milkin' in cow-ztall. Zoo in I went. 'Hetty, what about it now?' I zays. 'What about what?' 'er zaid, zticking 'er 'ead vurther into the cow, and jerkin' vast. 'Well,' I zays, 'begooin' to have I now?' 'Er waited half a minute and then 'er up and zaid, 'Mid's well I s'pose.' Zoo us got marr'd. 'Er 'ad a darn girt bride-ceake on the table adder the weddin', and 'er zhoved 'en across right in vront o' I. 'Here bist,' 'er zaid, 'I 'ooden gi' thee narry a bit last time, zoo thee cass eat's much as thee'st like now!' And I and Hetty hain't zpent narry a day apart zince then –'"

A sharp swish on the window from the lash of a whip caused both to gasp. 'Lar, thee needn't ha' vrightened the life out o'a body like that, John Sapseed,' rebuked his indignant mate, 'bezides what dost thee want roun' here this time o' addernoon?'

'I be zeein' 'bout ztartin' –

'Then theess'll have to ztart alone, vur I hain't told Mrs. Podger as 'ow Jeremiah Bunker went – '

'Now doant'ee be contrary, Jane, or us'll be late wi' the zeparatin' –

John gathered up the reins determinedly. – 'Be thee a-comin' – or be thee baint?' he demanded impatiently.

'Well, good addernoon, Mrs. Podger. I s'pose I better goo along wi' my perlite wold man,' were Mrs. Sapseed's parting words as she climbed into the waggon.

Dree Darset Men in Lon'on

The following was sent to the editor of the the *Dorset Year Book* by Stafford P Cox and published in 1914.

I'd bin a-thinken auver what the editor of the Dorset Year Book said about zenden along zummat for the magazine, an' it seemed to I that he midst like to hear how dree chaps from the wold County got on up his way. I know'd all o'em, an' they twold I all about it their very own zelves.

Oone o'em lived down to Piddletown. Now they be mighty sprack zart o' volk down there, an' they used to be turble fess cos they had a brass band an' tother villages haddent. Why, bless yer soul, they band-vellers got zoo blowed out wi' pride they were like girt drums!

An' every year they did have a outen all be theirzelves. Nothen ooden satisfy 'em oone time but they must goo to Lon'on.

In coos, the vust pleace to go to there wer th' Zoo. Ader they got tired o' looken at th' tother monkeys, what must 'em do but goo an' zee th' waxwork show at Madame Tussaud's. To git there they twold I they had t' walk athirt a girt park, an' zum o'em lost tothers. There zimed to be a goodish drong about, zoo they cooden vind em. But bimeby they come across a chap up on a box-like, a-talken to a middellenish crowd. Ader he'd a done, he zed, 'Friends, I shall be very pleased to answer any questions you mid like to ax.'

An' up speaks oone o' they Darset chaps, an a-zed, 'Mister, what I do want to know is, ev ee zeed any o' they there Piddletown band chaps about yer anywhere? About vivteen year back there wer a geamekeeper I know'd had to come droo Lon'on t'get to a town in Norfolk. I were liven down there then, an' I got in his carridge at our stashun, two or dree miles vrom where he wur gwain. He didden know I till I gidden a pwoke an' zed, "Well, Jack, how bist thee?"'

'Lawk a massy! Be that you? Where be I to now?'

'Oh! theest zoon be there; but theest got a worried look about ye; what's th' matter?'

'Oh', a zed, 'I be all in a caddle, vor I've lost me bag!'

'How's that?' zed I.

'Well, 'twere like this 'ere. I got to Liverpool Street 'bout oone o'clock, an' there wadden a train down thease way vor two mortal hours. Zoo I nabbed hold o' a porter an' zed to en, 'Mate, just look ader my bag, ool ee, while I d' teake a walk roun' the town.'

Well, I jist went vor a bit of a ramble, like, an' when I got back there wer noo porter an' noo bag! I be a-fear'd he took he whome along.'

'No,' I zed, 'I d' 'low he's in th' luggage van. What is er like?'

'Oh, oone o' they nice green carpet oones, wi' two leathern handles.'

'Did ee lock en up?'

'Oh, aye,' he zed, 'an' th' key were tied on th' handles!'

Then I had a wold vriend o' mine, Josiar Smith, down to Leigh. He twold I oonce how he went to Lon'on vor the vust time.

'Twere about aighteen varty-seven or aight' he zed. 'I wer putten up my hoss at The Antelope, at Darchester, oone day, an' th' ostler chap he zed to I, 'Be ee gwain be thic there scurshin train to-morrer, Mr. Smith?'

'What be that?' I zed.

'Why, thease yer new railway have a-got a jaunt up t'Lon'on an' back.'

'How do ee goo?' I zed.

'Oh, you do ax for a scurshin ticket at thic 'ere little wicket'like up to stashun, and pay yer feare, an' there you be.'

Zoo I ax'd two or dree young chaps down to Chetnole an' we 'greed to goo.

Next marnen, I putt on my best brown velveteen cwoat an' westcwoat, an' knee-breeches an' laggens, an my new beaver hat, an' zet out. We third-class volk had to ride in trucks-like, wi' low zides an' noo winders to en, but open at th' top. Th' zeats wer only planks just shaped up a mussel. We hadden drawed along many miles avore it ceame on to rain, an' we men-chaps took off our cwoats an' putt 'em round th' wimmen. Jarge Crumpler, he stood up oonce to'look ahead like, an' he got a girt zinder in his eye vrom th' engine vunnel. Zoo we tied he up wi' a red cotton handkercher. Th' engine wadden like they be now, cost they hatched en out dree or vower times to vill en up wi' water. Howsomdever, we got to Paddington at last, an' th' guard he knowed a pleace where we cou'd dry our cwoats an' get zummat t' eat. Ader that we zet out t' zee th' zights. Jarge he cum along a-blinken an' squinten out o' one eye, wi' to'other still tied up.

Well, I hadden gone vur avield avore I zeed a chap dressed jist like I was, an' zoo I said to myself, 'You bain't zoo vur out o' the' vashun then Josiar, though you ain't bin yer avore!'

Bimeby I crossed a street, an' jist az I got on the pavement, zure enough there wer another feller in velveteen an' breeches. I wer zo pleased I laffed at en an' touched the brim o' my beaver to en. Blowed if he didden do the same to I! An' twadden till a goodish bit ader that danged if I didden vind out that I was looken at mezelf all th' time in zum o' they girt new-vashuned plate-glass winders!

They were happy times, an' I hwope it will be many a year avore th' sons o' Darset lose their native simplicity of heart and freshness of outlook.

$\mathcal{T}$wo letters in dialect

The following is a copy of the invitation to the Tenth Annual Dinner of the Society of Dorset Men, held at a Holborn restaurant on May 4, 1914, which appeared in the *Dorset Year Book*, 1914-1915.

To the mampus (members) o' Do'set vo'k in Lon'on Town.

Dear Zur,

I do greet 'ee kindly, an' be in hopes that bist well an' hearty!

I be martel pleased to tell 'ee that our girt Yearly Veast 'ull be held again theas year, an' avorfe th' Tenth Time ov Axen, in the' King's Hall o' the Holborn Restaurant, on th' Vourth Day o' th' merry month o' May.

We be now, look zee, in double figgers, an', to keep it up praper-like, we be in mind to have a bright merry time o' it. Zoo come along, an' don't 'bide about on th' broad, or, when thou com'st, thou midst vind thy pleace a-took, vor which I should be ter'ble sorry.

Gie I thy neame an' thy dibs (Vive shilluns – every man Jack must fark out that, vor to pay vor th' vittles, let aloane th' drink). Gie em to I rathe, an' I'll zend 'ee back thy bit o' peastebwoard vor to let 'ee in.

The top man ov our vo'k, Zur Stephen Collins, who do zit in Cwoort an' also in th' Parliament House, 'all teake th' head pleace at th' Teable-bwoard. There'll be noo stint o' hearty cheer to munch. Zome good vo'k down Do'set way be a'gwain to send we zome blue-vinny cheese, nice and mwouldy, an' zome girt bowls o' cream vrom th' Blackmwore Veale vor to goo wi' th' Do'set viggety-pudden (meade by wold Robert Creedle in his best style!).

An', a'ter we've a-had our vill, mind'ee, we 'oont have too much speechifyin', no, od rabbit it if we 'ull. The speeches 'all be shart an' pithy, wi' a nice marrow o' wit to 'em. I warn 'ee, now, that Maister 'ull have a bit ov a bell – a good wold bell-metal tanket – an', if ar' a man do mouth on vor mwore 'n zix or seben minutes, he'll zound en; an' then, if er doon't let his clackers hrest vrom jabberin', oone ov our hefty men 'ull come up behin' em an' het en on top o' his crown wi' Bob creedle's hrollin pin! Noo, we be gwain to have zome merry zongs an' jokes, an' a kindly word wi' all our vriends.

Thease comes hoppin' it ull vind 'ee as it do leave I now. I do hope to hear vrom 'ee zoon that thou bist a-comin!

I be, as heretovwore, Thy true Vriend an' Servant,

William Watkins (Secretary)

Also from the *Dorset Year Book,* 1914-1915, is the following letter received by the secretary of the New Zealand branch of the Society of Dorset Men from a new arrival in the country, who had been put in touch with other Dorset immigrants.

Dear Zur,

I be writin' for to tell 'ee how grateful I be for puttin' us on the track of the Do'set men out here an' I would like to zay they be jist zo hearty out here, as they be in the wold pleace.

No zooner'n the boat were alongside the wharf at Wellin'ton up comes good Mweaster Moore on the gangway, almost a'fore h'ed a-touched the zide an' gied us a real good Do'set welcome. An' after w'ed a-pitched our vew traps an' had a look roun', he come roun' to the pleace where we were stoppin' for the night an' ax us to come roun' to zee his good wife.

Well a-vore we'd a-ben there very long, in drawed oone vrom Sherborne an another vrom Poole and oone or two vrom Do'chester, until be danged there were a house vull o'volk. Then oone het up a tune on the pianner an' then we had a zong or two. Oone o' em zung thik zong Mr. Galpin put together, an' then to cap all in come Measter Moore in a wold smock an' hat, wie a hoe in his hand, and het up thik wold zong, 'The Turmit Hoer.'

Well I thought this is a bit o' Do'set if you minded, an' we all o' us het into the chorus that the neighbours must have thought that there were a weddin' or a christenin' or zummit.

Well, Zur, I be jist telling o' ee this for ee to zee that its jist like comin' vrom whome to whome when you do come to a strange land and vind such a welcome a-waiting o' ee.

An', bless thee zoul, their kindness did'n stop there. But they must put their heads together an' twold us the best pleace to look vor a job. An' we took their advice, an' bwoth o' us (Meader and self) have vell into good jobs.

Then vor Do'set dear we'll gie oone cheer, 'ye hear, oone cheer.

Yours faithfully,

(signed) Wm. BARNETT
Dannevirke, Hawkes Bay, New Zealand.

ACKNOWLEDGEMENTS

I am indebted to *A Glossary of the Dorset Dialect* by William Barnes.

I am also grateful to the following:

Beau Parke, for permission to use an extract from *From the Lower Garden Gate*, 1999

Dr Stevens-Cox, literary executor of J Stevens-Cox, for permission to quote from *Dorset Dishes of the 17th Century.*

A J Blad, for permission to use the photograph of the Dairy House at Bloxworth.

Nigel J Clarke Publications, for permission to use the photograph of Dorset Apple Cake.

Devina Symes, for her poem, *Darzet Volk,* and for the loan of her photograph of William Barnes.

Dorset County Library, for use of the photograph of *The King Rewarding the Industrious Haymaker,* and five other photographs: *Harvesting at Sturminster Marshall; Thatching; The Hangman's Cottage, Dorchester; Maypole, Sturminster Marshall; The Wishing Well at Upwey.*

The publishers of *Dorset Year Book,* and to my friend, the late George Lanning (editor 1995-2000), for his valued help and advice.

ABOUT THE AUTHOR

Jean Bellamy was born in London but has lived in Dorset for most of her life, first at Poole and for the last sixteen years in Weymouth. Her writing career started in 1970 and eight years later, having given up full-time secretarial work, she was able to devote more of her time to contributing articles and short stories to a wide variety of publications. Full-length fiction – three novels for children, all with west country settings – and five Dorset non-fiction books followed. Research for *Dorset as she wus Spoke* has led her to an even greater appreciation of Dorset's famous poet, schoolmaster and clergyman, William Barnes, and to a fascination with the Dorset dialect.